THE SNOW PALACE

Pam Gems

THE SNOW PALACE

OBERON BOOKS
LONDON

First published in 1998 by Oberon Books Ltd.
(incorporating Absolute Classics)
521 Caledonian Road, London N7 9RH
Tel: 0171 607 3637 / Fax: 0171 607 3629
e-mail: oberon.books@btinternet.com

British Library Cataloguing-in-Publication-Data
A catalogue record for this book is available from the British
Library.

ISBN 1 84002 065 2

Cover design: TM ltd

Typography: Richard Doust

Printed in Great Britain by Antony Rowe Ltd., Reading.

Contents

INTRODUCTION

Pam Gems

I n the early 1980s I was asked by the RSC to look at a script written by a Polish writer Stanislawa Przybyszewska (her name, she wrote, was the butt of jokes in her own country). It was intriguing. A woman playwright, that rare species, working in the 20s. Facts revealed a unique story. Stanislawa, it turned out, was the illegitimate daughter of Stanislaw Przybyszewsky, avant-garde writer, wild man, drinker, reputed Satanist, friend of Strindberg and Edvard Munch. Her mother, Aniela Pajak, was a painter, who lived unconventionally. In later girlhood Stanislawa lived with her Aunt, Helena.

As a girl, she conceived a passion for the French Revolution and, in particular, for Maximilien Robespierre, Marat's 'Sea-Green Incorruptible', the man of 'vertu'; the man who believed in the civic imperative, of the absolute need for human beings to care for one another. It is possible that the rackety nature of her own background attracted Stanislawa to the notion of balance and decency as the ethics for life. At all events she shortened her skirts, cut her hair (the Great War having killed off the men, girls were now required to have boyish haircuts and no breasts), embraced communism and began to write. She tried a book, then switched to a dramatic version of the French Revolution. This ran to 600 pages. It is a strange piece of work, rambling, passionate, more of a film than a stage play. The focus is uncertain, the writing in parts abreactive, probably because she was on morphine. The lack of experience shows. Playwriting is a practical craft, shaped, sometimes released, by exigency. She became increasingly reclusive, eventually choosing to live in an unheated school hut in Gdansk. When it became clear that a production of her play was unlikely, she began to write long letters to people such as Thomas Mann, people she felt to be her intellectual peers.

Most of these letters were never sent, and are regarded nowadays as the best and most interesting of her oeuvre.

The RSC said to have a look, that Andrzej Wajda had clawed a movie out of the material. The film was wonderful, a dangerous tilt at the then regime in Poland, with the Polish actor, Pzoniak, who looks like General Jaruzelski, as a repressive Robespierre, and the young Gérard Depardieu incomparable as Danton. A hard act to follow. It was suggested that I might prefer to write a play of my own on the French Revolution. Perhaps, after all, that would be the better artistic solution. Which, of course, was impossible. This was Stanislawa's, not mine, although coincidentally, I'd had a weakness for Danton for years, and a picture of his ugly mug hung halfway up the stairs. I went to Warsaw, where Solidarity was alive and vibrant, saw the grave of Father Popieluszko – recently murdered by the regime – where mass was played on tape 24 hours a day, and you could smell the flowers, as at Kensington Palace, streets away. The shops were empty of food and consumer goods, people queued in the streets for a few withered oranges. I came back and cut the play from 600 to 100 pages and it was produced in the Barbican in '85.

But. During the cutting, carving and shaping, what became intriguing, dramatically beguiling, was the shadowy figure of Stanislawa herself. She wrote of her isolation, and of the ecstasy of creative work. The parallels between her life – lived, as an artist, to the utmost – and the lives of the revolutionaries Robespierre and Danton, prepared to commit everything, each with a fervent political agenda (the notion of Left and Right began with the Revolution) – these parallels seemed so cogent. Where do we strike the balance between the hedonistic and the ascetic? Where there are two possible rights, problems arise. Which path to take for the civic good? All decision to act is a gamble. Radical politics, connoting change, can only offer promise, pledge. And change can be fatally easy. Simplicity itself to dismantle, less easy to reconstruct. Should a reforming government go hell for leather, the whole hog? Or temporise, tread softly. Do we accept as constant the 'realities' of realpolitik... the domination of the market... concede that the world is run by the gamble of the stock market and relationships cemented around the banqueting table? Or do we, if in government, see our function as holding in tension, in balance, the rights, responsibilities and privileges of citizens, of the people? Danton says give them peace and prosperity and no government interference – power of the periphery, true democracy. Robespierre, the man of 'vertu', stands by the absolute necessity of responsible citizenship. For the maintenance of a conscious sense of community, based on the notion of service. A life shaped only by commerce and self-interest, he says, 'leads to bestiality and the rape of children.'

I became fascinated by Stanislawa's fascination. And by her. She died, in the end, of hypothermia, in her thirties, in her unheated hut, leaving notes of her travail as she began to freeze to death. 'To the utmost' killed her, as it did Danton and Robespierre. Nonetheless, despite reaction, they gave the world an incomparable push forward from medievalism and the despotic to the rule of law and the rights of man. Not an unimportant subject to be obsessed by. Passionately misguided? Foolishly self-destructive? I would say a brave, lonely woman. A pathfinder. Pathfinders get picked off. They command our respect.

Pam Gems
London, 1998

Characters

STANISLAWA PRZYBYSZEWSKA

MOTHER/AUNT HELENA

FATHER/DANTON

ROBESPIERRE

SAINT-JUST/WAITER

ANNA/LOUISE/WOMAN

The Snow Palace was first performed at the Wilde Theatre, Bracknell on 22nd January 1998 and toured the UK for eight weeks with the following cast:

ST JUST, Justin Avoth
MOTHER/AUNT HELENA/WOMAN, Kristin Milward
STANISLAWA, Kathryn Pogson
ROBESPIERRE, Kenn Sabberton
ANNA/LOUISE, Jemma Shaw
DANTON/FATHER, Robert Willox

The London premiere was at the Tricycle Theatre on 1st December 1998, with the following cast:

ST JUST, Justin Avoth
ROBESPIERRE, Nigel Cooke
DANTON/FATHER, Mark Lewis Jones
MOTHER/AUNT HELENA/WOMAN, Kristin Milward
STANISLAWA, Kathryn Pogson
ANNA/LOUISE, Katrina Syran

Director, Janet Suzman
Designer, Bruce Macadie
Sound designer, John A. Leonard for Aura
Lighting designer, Ian Scott
Produced by The Sphinx Theatre Company

ACT ONE

The interior of a wooden hut. It is extremely poorly furnished with almost no furniture. What there is is broken or impoverished. There is a small black stove with a pipe and a window which is half-draped with a ragged orange cardigan. The small panes of the window are so thick with frost that the light from outside is obscured.

A woman is writing at a small kitchen table. She is very thin, with darkish hair roughly cropped in the style of the Twenties. It is hard to tell her age. She writes swiftly, hunched over the table, her hands cramped with the cold. Voice in on the P/A.

STANISLAWA: ... nonsense, a lie, untrue... (*Looks round briefly, shivers without noticing from the cold.*) ... to the contrary, I'm very comfortable. My room here in the school grounds is small, as you saw, but for my purpose it is superb, everything I could desire... anonymous, neutral, for a writer the perfect hermitage so dearest, dearest Aunt, will you please – please stop worrying about my health and sanity... as you see – I have survived! I am, as the English say, in the pink so less, less, less of the cat with the drowned kitten... on second thoughts, continue to be concerned for your highly intelligent, deeply talented and wholly adoring niece... Stanislawa.

STANISLAWA finishes writing, puts down the pen then picks it up again to add a postscript.

STANISLAWA: How is the old man, still dispensing charity to those above him? Damn him! – buy the skirt! My heart is yours.

She puts the letter into an envelope, makes to lick the seal, adds another postscript.

STANISLAWA: (*Voice-over.*) My play is going well. What do you mean, what subject? Naturellement, my beloved Robespierre! – who else?

She straightens up and stretches stiffly, pulling her arms wide and easing her shoulders, something she does throughout. She seals the envelope, addresses it, and, as another afterthought, turns it over and scrawls on the back.

STANISLAWA: I – am – well.

She stands, the sealed letter in her hand, white-faced with the cold. Looks about vaguely then, propping the letter up on the table, crosses to the stove. Shivering, she picks up an old battered enamel saucepan from the top of the stove and crosses to the door. Opening it, we see white snowdrifts. She disappears outside, and returns with the saucepan piled high with snow. This she tries to melt on the stove but it is not warm enough. She finds a candle end, looks for matches and lights it, with difficulty, with a twist of old newspaper poked into the stove. She puts the lit candle under a tripod, rests the saucepan on the top and looks for wood for the fire. She finds a few pieces and puts them into the stove. She returns and stirs the snow until it melts. She sips the water from the pan, wincing at the coldness, and walks about, pan in hand, sipping.

As she does so there is the sound of a woman laughing, low, on the P/A.

STANISLAWA paces, sipping. The WOMAN laughs again, closer. Further off a man begins to protest mildly.

ROBESPIERRE: (*Voice-over.*) Not now, Léo... no, no, no!... Eléonore!

The WOMAN's laughter, low and close and seductive.

STANISLAWA: (*Voice-over.*) Oh we know what You think, my dear Robespierre!

She imitates his dry voice and precise diction, goes to her table.

STANISLAWA: (*Voice-over.*) "Manifestations of love during the daylight are in the worst possible taste!"

ROBESPIERRE: Did I say that?

STANISLAWA bends over the table, writing rapidly.

ROBESPIERRE: (*Laughs gently.*) Fine principles from a fit man. From a weak wreck, less persuasive.

STANISLAWA: On the contrary, my dear, you're obviously recovering. Alas.

ROBESPIERRE: You'd rather have me on my back?

STANISLAWA: Eléonore, sadly – At least I see you then. (*Looks at the page, pencil between her teeth.*) ... at least I see you then... I see you then... (*Chews the end of the pencil.*)

ROBESPIERRE enters in a dressing gown.

ROBESPIERRE: My poor Eléonore...

At the loving concern in his voice STANISLAWA half-turns in her chair with an involuntary spasm of anguish. She pulls an ugly face, dismissing the feeling.

ROBESPIERRE: My dear. I'm sorry. (*A groaning sigh.*) I really believed it. A year of intense revolutionary work, then back to privacy and you... instead of which... (*ROBESPIERRE exits.*)

STANISLAWA: Instead of which I'm becoming nothing but a huge, inflamed Brain and – ach!

She nearly jumps out of her skin at a rat-a-tat-tat on her door. She swings herself back against the wall so that she cannot be seen by anyone looking in at the window.

ANNA: (*Calls from without in a child's falsetto, her form of greeting.*) Ooo-ah! Ooo-ah!

STANISLAWA, rigid against the wall, pulls a vicious face. She edges further away. Sounds of scraping as ANNA gets a foothold, sounds of scratching as she clears a pane of glass, and peers in the window.

ANNA: Hullo, Hullo... anyone in? It's Anna, your neighbour. May I come in?

STANISLAWA keeps still. Scraping sounds as ANNA keeps a foothold, then the characteristic knock once more... rat-a-tat-tat.

ANNA: Hullo?

Silence. Then sounds of ANNA's departure. STANISLAWA, bent double to stay below the line of the window, creeps back to the table and slides into her seat. But her concentration has been dented. She sits, raking her neck back and forth like an angry fowl, muttering to herself. She pulls herself together with a visible effort.

STANISLAWA: (*Through her teeth.*) Not... important. (*Released, her mind drifts back to her work.*) Not important. (*A sudden decision.*) Get her off. (*She picks up her pencil, bends over the page, mutters to herself.*) Farewell, Eléonore.

On the P/A the same rat-a-tat-tat at the door.

STANISLAWA: And enter... the Angel of Death... the baleful... Saint-Just!

ST. JUST's voice louder as he approaches.

ST. JUST: (*Voice-over.*) Citizen Robespierre is out of bed? Bravo – my God, do I smell coffee?

His voice is close on the last word and STANISLAWA groans at the word 'coffee'. She rises, crosses, burrows among empty tins. No coffee. She smells an empty tin for its fragrance, sliding back quickly into her seat, anxious not to lose her thread as ST. JUST enters.

ST. JUST: (*Turning behind him.*) We should have arrested every malcontent, madman and rogue six months ago... as it is, God knows what's going to happen.

ROBESPIERRE enters, looking frail. Like ST. JUST, he carries a lot of paper.

ROBESPIERRE: (*Light.*) I thought you'd abolished God – oh, now you're annoyed with me.

ST. JUST: My feelings are neither here nor there, they don't enter into it, although I do, as you know, feel most strongly that we should remove totems and medieval magic from the people if they are to march forward –

ROBESPIERRE: All right, all right, all right... sorry, I've been away from... from your wonderful energy, my dear.

ST. JUST: It's been the devil without you. People slide! A few setbacks, all of a sudden this man's left Paris, or the country, others change hats, the pettiness of the squabbles you wouldn't believe! There's a weird cynicism about – well we all know where that comes from.

ROBESPIERRE: Oh, not again!

ST. JUST: You haven't been here... you've been ill. When I tried to tell you of new alliances, people switching sides overnight, you were jittering with fever. He never stops!

ROBESPIERRE: That's his style! Like you, he has this wonderful vitality. I wish I'd half –

ST. JUST: I am insulted to be coupled with Georges Danton.

ROBESPIERRE: Anton. The man is a colleague. A different sort of man, that's all. No less relevant, we all want the same –

ST. JUST: No, no, and no. What he wants is your place. He's got the streets behind him but that isn't enough and he knows it. He needs the respect and trust that is yours, that you have earned by what you do, by who you are. He wants to be you!

ROBESPIERRE: Oh I doubt if Danton would change places.

ST. JUST: He wants to sit where you sit. He'll kill for it.

ROBESPIERRE: That – is a very dangerous accusation to make of a colleague and a brave man. (*He rises, frigid, frightening.*)

ST. JUST: (*Stammers.*) I'm sorry.

ROBESPIERRE: You are destructive.

ST. JUST: I'm sorry, I'm sorry. It's the truth, should I keep it to myself? I smell it, I honestly believe you're in danger – physical danger. Maxime, these are not normal days.

ROBESPIERRE: And you think he wants to put a knife in my back? That he's capable of murder? Well do you?

ST. JUST: All I know is that I'd die for you.

ROBESPIERRE: Rubbish – stop it. I will not be an icon to replace the pietas you're ripping from the altars of France. We'll have less talk of violence – violence is for despots and criminals. If there is one achievement we may hope for in this unprecedented...

ST. JUST: Struggle?

ROBESPIERRE: ... enterprise... endeavour... it is to emerge from brutish medievalism. You *must* learn to stop fighting. Learn to persuade. You want me to muzzle Danton? What are you talking about, he's our link with the people, he's one of them.

ST. JUST: No he isn't. Any more than we are.

ROBESPIERRE: We are educated men who have responded to the need for human justice.

ST. JUST: From – nonetheless – positions of privilege.

ROBESPIERRE: And Georges Danton is abusing that privilege? That's what you're saying.

ST. JUST: The whole of Paris knows it. The man's corrupt – it's common knowledge.

ROBESPIERRE: We need him.

ST. JUST: Because we can control the mob? And who controls Danton? The more you indulge him, the more his ambition swells – he thinks you condone! I say cut him down while it is still possible.

ROBESPIERRE: (*Sharp.*) No!

ST. JUST: Why this sudden reluctance to shed blood?

ROBESPIERRE: (*Incisive.*) We need him.

ST. JUST: What do you want – proof? I'll get it for you. (*He exits.*)

ROBESPIERRE sweeps up his papers from his desk, leaves. STANISLAWA utters a shuddering groan.

STANISLAWA: Ohhh!

The pencil falls from her frozen hand. She staggers, and reels, lurches to her feet unsteadily. She stamps her stiff legs, and walks up and down to get back feeling. She crosses to the window.

STANISLAWA: Snow, damn you!

She finds a sack and drapes it over her shoulders, clutching it to her. She puts more wood on the stove, squats on the floor, hunched as close to the fire as she can and goes into stupor.

STANISLAWA: Mamushu... Mamoo... (*Murmurs.*) ... I'm cold... Mamoo! I'm cold!

Her MOTHER enters, a tall, handsome woman with a scarf wrapped about her head, pinned with a large jet brooch. She searches, finds a bottle of vodka, looks about for a glass.

STANISLAWA: (*Matter of fact.*) You told me my Father was a big Swede.

MOTHER: (*Absently, busying herself with the bottle.*) No-o, I just said that.

STANISLAWA: What for? Why? Why will you never tell me?

MOTHER: (*Irritable, unable to open the bottle.*) I don't know, what does it matter?

She gets the top off, pours herself a drink and savours the first mouthful.

STANISLAWA: Why him? Why a Swede?

Her MOTHER shrugs, pulling a face, just like her daughter.

STANISLAWA: (*Grumpy.*) I've been reading Swedish history!

Her MOTHER, after another swallow, sits, placated, undoing her jacket. She belches discreetly.

STANISLAWA: I thought I might be descended from Queen Christina of Sweden... royal! (*She pulls a silly face.*)

MOTHER: You could have been! – well, if he *had* been a Swede, your Father.

STANISLAWA: Don't be silly. If it wasn't him who was it? Or were there so many you can't remember? Tell me about him.

MOTHER: Who?

STANISLAWA: My Father!

MOTHER: That lecher.

STANISLAWA: Lecher? Who is he, what's he like?

MOTHER: You'll get nothing there.

STANISLAWA: Who is he? What does he look like?...
is he handsome?

MOTHER: No... ugly. (*STANISLAWA groans.*) I should stay
clear if I were you – he's killed more than once.

STANISLAWA: You chose well.

MOTHER: I know! Sorry. (*Apologetically.*) I did *try* to get rid
of you.

STANISLAWA gives her a dry look.

STANISLAWA: Is he Polish?

MOTHER: Yes.

STANISLAWA: So, a madman. What's his name?

MOTHER: Przybyszewsky. The bastard.

STANISLAWA: No. I'm the bastard. (*Joking.*) Not Stanislaw
Przybyszewsky?

MOTHER: Yes that's him.

STANISLAWA: You don't mean Przybyszewsky the
dramatist, the novelist, the friend of Edvard Munch –
Strindberg – all those avant-garde artists, you mean?

MOTHER: Yes.

STANISLAWA: You mean I'm his daughter?

MOTHER: Yes!

STANISLAWA: I'm the daughter of Stanislaw
Przybyszewsky?

MOTHER: (*Shrieks.*) Yes!!

STANISLAWA: I don't believe it. (*She stands, dumbfounded.*) Are you sure?

MOTHER: (*Groans, then.*) Yes.

STANISLAWA: I'm the daughter of a famous man. I'm Przybyszewsky's daughter.

Her FATHER enters – fondles the MOTHER's breasts.

The significance of her Christian name penetrates.

STANISLAWA: Stanislaw... Stanislawa!

She stands before her mother, beaming idiotically with pure happiness. She is unaware of her FATHER.

MOTHER: I shouldn't get too ecstatic if I were you. You're not his only bastard.

STANISLAWA: I've got a Father.

Her MOTHER looks ironically up at her FATHER, but he is otherwise engaged with her bosom.

STANISLAWA: I've got a famous, brilliant man for my Father!

She wheels on her MOTHER.

STANISLAWA: (*Hoarse shout.*) Hey!!

This makes her MOTHER jump.

STANISLAWA: Why didn't you say he was my Father! What happened?

The FATHER grips her MOTHER's throat as a casual reminder of his dominance.

STANISLAWA: Did he leave you or did you leave him? Was it because of me?

The FATHER saunters off, with a backward glance at the MOTHER as he puts on his slouch hat. The MOTHER retches a little, feeling her throat, recovers.

MOTHER: Can't remember – leave it... who cares!

She puts on lipstick, adjusts the scarf on her head, leaves without farewell.

STANISLAWA stands, then shudders. She pulls herself free of memory, crosses, reaches for her large notebook and turns the pages for her place, strolls, reading.

STANISLAWA: Cold. Wet. A third bad harvest. Paris runs out of bread. The Queen, Marie-Antoinette, asks for fine flour, brioche flour, to be released for sale to the poor to ease their hunger, is damned illogically by History for supposedly saying: 'Let them eat cake.'

At the word 'cake' STANISLAWA gives a little groan, forages for food. Eats a piece of bread.

1789. Suddenly, everywhere, people are on the streets. They storm the Bastille, let out a few surprised old prisoners and the Rights of Man are agreed and declared. (*She chuckles to herself.*)

1790. The first government of the people set up, swept forward by Maximilien Robespierre – Marat's "Sea-Green Incorruptible" – and the man with the roar, smiling Georges Danton, lawyer, lecher... and the people's idol.

1791. King Louis makes a run for it, is recognised from his coins and hauled back to Paris with the Queen.

1792. The whole world... except America... hostile. France stands alone.

STANISLAWA, by the window, hears her name called over the sound of the wind as a snowstorm blows up.

MOTHER: (*Offstage.*) Stashoo... Stashoo......

STANISLAWA slips her coat off as the door blows open. The MOTHER stands there. She looks dreadfully ill. STANISLAWA helps her to lie down on a truckle bed. The MOTHER is suddenly, violently, and noisily sick. STANISLAWA, whose actions reveal that she is used to this, is ready with an enamel bowl at once, fetches newspaper, cloths, and cleans up the mess. She puts a cover over her MOTHER to keep her warm, gives her medicine and sits by her side, to tend her.

MOTHER: You'll miss school.

STANISLAWA: Doesn't matter.

Her MOTHER moans softly.

MOTHER: God I feel bad.

STANISLAWA sits by her, motionless. The light goes. STANISLAWA lights a candle.

MOTHER: (*Murmurs, in her sleep.*) Oh dear... oh dear...

STANISLAWA: (*Comforting her.*) Sssh...

MOTHER: I haven't been much of a Mother.

STANISLAWA: Doesn't matter.

MOTHER: I used to leave you in the car...

STANISLAWA: With a bag of liquorice.

MOTHER: Somebody said it was good for kids. (*She drifts off.*) Why can't I have a good time, what's wrong with it? HE used to say... 'there's nobody up there, do as you want'... (*She shudders suddenly.*) Only what he wanted was torture. And then laugh at the blood.

STANISLAWA: What?!

STANISLAWA backs away, horrified. Her MOTHER mumbles, then beckons feebly. STANISLAWA leans close. Her MOTHER strokes STANISLAWA's face briefly.

MOTHER: (*Becoming indistinct.*) Don't trust him. Go to your Aunt in Cracow. She'll look after...

STANISLAWA: But I want to meet my Father.

MOTHER: No. No. Ask Helena, she'll tell you – oh Christ!

She heaves, as if to be sick, but the spasm subsides. STANISLAWA rises, with the bowl.

MOTHER: (*Weak.*) Don't move the bowl, Stashoo.

STANISLAWA sits again, by her MOTHER. She blows out the candle. Lights down. The MOTHER exits.

STANISLAWA: (*Calls.*) Mamoo! (*Puts on a jacket.*)

The lights come up, warmer. STANISLAWA, with renewed energy, paces with her book, reading her notes.

STANISLAWA: Spring... 1794. Robespierre recovering from malaria, Danton back in Paris, fresh from his new country estates and the young body of his child bride. St. Just tables a motion for a Rule of Terror – to be limited to times of crisis.

(*She sits to write.*) The imposition of Terror... (*She looks up, thinking.*) ... the imposition of Terror...

ST. JUST: (*Offstage.*) The imposition of Terror... (*Enters.*) ... is an act of cauterization.

STANISLAWA: (*Murmurs.*) ... cauterization...

ST. JUST: It is designed to eradicate vicious elements.

ROBESPIERRE: (*Enters.*) The fanatics of the Cordelier Club are the problem. At least you can't accuse *Danton* of extremism.

ST. JUST: (*Puts papers before ROBESPIERRE.*) Only because it's not in his interest. He's growing like a fungus! With foreign support non-existent, bread running out again, our brother revolutionary, seeing the pickings dwindle, not only sucks every tit his fat hands can squeeze, but begins to spread reaction!

ROBESPIERRE: (*Reading.*) Are these accurate?

ST. JUST: Yes.

ROBESPIERRE: Reliable sources?

ST. JUST: Your own people.

Silence. ROBESPIERRE rises slowly.

ST. JUST: They must be arrested, today, all of them – including Danton.

ROBESPIERRE: (*Rises, speaks dreamily, looking out of the window.*) I'm fond of Georges. Doesn't do to let him know – he takes advantage.

ST. JUST: (*Stabs at the papers on the table.*) Proof of fraud. Proof of embezzlement. Proof, written and witnessed, of treason to the state, by secret treaties with foreign powers.

ROBESPIERRE: (*Looks up into ST. JUST's face.*) The people's champion on trial?

ST. JUST: You're saying Danton's above the law? A woman out there who hoards a loaf of bread has her head chopped off.

ROBESPIERRE: Not if she has the popular support enjoyed by our adored revolutionary, Danton. I have to say that in an open fight –

ST. JUST: In an open fight you'd carry the Convention before you nem con!

ROBESPIERRE: My dear Antoine... how young you are.

ST. JUST: It is not a matter of experience but of fact – and conviction.

ROBESPIERRE: (*Sharp.*) Then I must tell you that at this time my conviction is for a delayed decision on the matter of Danton.

ST. JUST: Have you got a temperature?

ROBESPIERRE: No.

ST. JUST: You're afraid of him.

ROBESPIERRE: No.

ST. JUST: I think you are.

ROBESPIERRE: (*Turns on him.*) No! I am afraid of the horror we shall release if we split into faction. Do you think we can waste energy in internal wrangling? You think That's the way forward for France?

ST. JUST: Maxime... in the name of justice...

ROBESPIERRE: Justice? My dear Antoine, I hardly think that is a luxury in which we may indulge ourselves. For the present. Nor will I permit the fatally easy course of your reign of Terror. That is for thugs.

ST. JUST: (*Throws himself down, sulky.*) What then?

ROBESPIERRE: For the sake of our souls, I shall compromise.

ST. JUST: Compromise? With that lecher?

STANISLAWA: (*Murmurs, frowning.*) Lecher?

ROBESPIERRE: With our revolutionary co-patriot, Danton. I shall arrange a meeting.

ST. JUST: The whole of Paris will gloat, they'll assume he's suborned you... you'll be seen as complicit, weak, if nothing worse...

ROBESPIERRE: Oh my dear, what are humiliations when the future of the Republic is at stake? I doubt the necessity to kiss Danton's shoe but... should France demand it of me... (*They go.*)

During the above a trio plays Mozart. A low buzz of voices, and clatter of cutlery. DANTON enters, cutting off sound as he shuts the door. Dressed floridly for evening he inspects the laid dining table. He makes a few changes, puts the chairs closer, sniffs the wine, pays off the hovering WAITER who bows and goes. He helps himself to a drink, tries the food.

ROBESPIERRE enters soundlessly.

DANTON: Maxime!... good to see you! How are you feeling, I hear you've been ill!

ROBESPIERRE: I hear *you've* been having me followed.

DANTON: For your own protection! (*Shepherds ROBESPIERRE to a seat.*) We all know who's the heart and engine of this great endeavour of ours. The intellect of France! – always were, never knew a case brought to court you didn't read clear.

ROBESPIERRE: And sometimes lose against you.

DANTON: (*Eating.*) Only because I made them feel sorry for me. 'Here comes old Georges with his big ugly mug, making a mess of it again.'

ROBESPIERRE: A most inaccurate appraisal. As you know.

DANTON: It helped to smile a lot.

ROBESPIERRE: You recommend false demeanour in court.

DANTON: We're talking about the law, not justice!

ROBESPIERRE: Touché.

DANTON: Not that *your* face is your best friend.

ROBESPIERRE: I've never pretended to beauty!

DANTON: Only the best-looking man in Paris. That profile! (*Despite himself, ROBESPIERRE preens.*) But so open! Not always in the client's interest, d'you see? Honest aspect, yes. But not necessarily conveying dictionary, thesaurus and almanack at a glance. Those eyes! Like an ocean, signalling every hour of the tide... slack, full, dangerous ebb. A handicap for a lawyer. In a politician, downright frightening... (*Shudders.*)

ROBESPIERRE: I *frighten* you?

DANTON: Maxime – I'm frightened *for* you.

ROBESPIERRE: I see. What do you suggest I do to protect myself?

DANTON: (*Laughs.*) Come on! You won't catch me there! No lawyer asks a question to which he don't know the answer. We ain't in court now.

ROBESPIERRE: (*He suddenly seems tired, ill.*) What do you want?

DANTON: You know what I want – your friendship! Trust! (*He leans forward, tucks a rug around ROBESPIERRE's knees with loving skill.*) That's better. You shouldn't be out – she's not looking after you properly. They're all the same, these women, they like us on our backs, oh, we'll take care of you, what they want is to colonise us, story of Samson eh... only it isn't our hair they want to cut off... sit still... (*He picks up a spoon.*) It's just a little fortified meat soup, it won't harass the digestion – you must recover your strength – for the sake of France! (*So ROBESPIERRE takes the soup.*) I should have been here, seeing to you, instead of... (*He sighs.*) ... tell you the truth I'm exhausted. We've been through too much. Responsibility for life, death – the sights we've seen!... it binds you together. Those who haven't been where we have... God knows I never sought high place... no, takes it out of you... (*He spoons the soup.*)

ROBESPIERRE: Your courage has been a lamp to us all.

He lifts his hand, DANTON puts down the spoon, pours a glass of wine. ROBESPIERRE watches him, deft with bottle, glass and snowy napkin.

ROBESPIERRE: I have always admired you. Your voice, booming through chambers, across courtyards... that enormous laugh like the thunder of gods... your capacity for... camaraderie...

He accepts the glass of wine, drinks at DANTON's smiling encouragement. Puts down the glass.

ROBESPIERRE: I have never acquired a facility for living.

DANTON: You should try it. Nothing wrong with enjoyment.

ROBESPIERRE: In its proper place.

DANTON: I agree. Question of balance. Like the law... based on what's reasonable. Too much this way, no good... too much that way – disaster. If you get my meaning.

ROBESPIERRE: Your point?

DANTON: Retrenchment. Withdraw from extreme measures. For the sake of us all... your head as well as mine. We're offering devoted loyalty, total support.

ROBESPIERRE: (*Pause.*) I have reports of your faction. In all the years that we have shared acquaintance it never occurred to me that Georges Danton, professional colleague, fellow-revolutionary and brother-in-arms, was as rotten as a dead stick on the forest floor.

DANTON: What? What?

ROBESPIERRE throws a piece of paper to him.

ROBESPIERRE: I also have my spies. This revolution –
if it survives – will survive through, and only through
the most stringent sacrifice and devoted service. And
by example.

DANTON: They love me!

ROBESPIERRE: D'you think the bourgeoisie, our new
backbone... the farmers, journeymen... d'you think the
Sans-Culottes will follow you to the barricades for
Collusion? That they have such a low opinion of
themselves? You think people live by the Deal? By
mere transaction? By the banality of trade?

DANTON: By God, there are worse ways to live. The law
of contract, my friend, has a great deal to recommend
it. Trade is the way forward.

ROBESPIERRE: (*His voice shrill.*) Insufficient! To live by
transaction alone ends in greed – fraud – criminality. In
the withering of the soul. In bestiality. In the rape of
children.

Silence.

DANTON: (*Low and murderous.*) My marriage is a love
match.

ROBESPIERRE: Would you have got her without your
money and position? I'm sorry. But you must see.
Without the backbone of morality, society cannot hold
any more than this. (*He smashes his hand down on a jelly,
lifts it, shining red like blood.*) Where's the resistance?
Every man for himself ? Can that create a nation with
heart, pride, identity – self-respect?

Silence. DANTON scans the piece of paper with the charges.

31

DANTON: (*Looks up at last.*) As to finance – I should never have been left to my own devices, I needed assistance... and with the war councils and the edicts and instructions from the Committees and your office... you've overloaded us all! Change everything? In a year?! Impose democracy... fight foreign wars, de-Christianise – all right, we pulled back there on your advice... yes – I agree! 'Fairness for all'... but when the harvests fail, how are we to achieve even one crust a day apiece, tell me that.

You want free education, poor relief, money for widows, free medical treatment for all... Maxime! On paper – divine! The most inspired humanity the world has ever dreamed of. But within a year?

Is it surprising that we fail you?

All right, I've slipped.

I do my best – yes, there has been error. But no malice, I've always been your man... dammit, we stand for the same thing, how can we be enemies?

Maxime......

Please...

Make me the Mayor of Boulogne – I'll leave tonight, with my little woman. To tell the truth I'd be happier – I'll take my girl and go, with your blessing – serve France in whatever –

ROBESPIERRE: Impossible! You know that. Leave now, you leave chaos and a total loss of morale behind you. In times of crisis the Committee of Security must have support from all, I repeat, every faction. There must be discipline.

DANTON: I'll account for every penny of this. We'll make fresh arrangements, my people and yours. A new entente.

ROBESPIERRE: Would you be good enough to sign to that?

DANTON: Oh, Maxime! Maxime! You never needed to worry about old Georges! My dick's in your back pocket, surely you know that? Mind you... you're asking us to sign our death warrants.

ROBESPIERRE: What?

DANTON: Anything that's possible – I'm your man, but... change human nature? Abolish crime? You might as well try and stop us all pissing!

People work for one thing – themselves! You think they'll do it for virtue – where's the profit in that now we've abolished God and the Hereafter? (*Laughs.*)

ROBESPIERRE: The soul of man is –

DANTON: The soul of man? Testicles! Why are they with us, that rabble out there, I'll tell you... because we promise a better share-out... and what's wrong with that? The freedom to be a self-supporting unit – that's democracy. Every man for himself... human nature, Maxime... human nature! Pull back. We've gone far enough. (*Drunk, his attention begins to go.*) Too much blood in the streets – the stink's devaluing property.

ROBESPIERRE: Rich – coming from you.

DANTON: Necessary measures. All right – it got out of hand. Unleash the mob, they want revenge.

(*Pause.*) Maxime – you and I, we could rule the world together. It's our destiny. Men aren't created equal, never will be.

ROBESPIERRE: There is a natural virtue in every man that asks only –

DANTON: (*Laughs.*) The only virtue I know is what I put into my wife's little hole three times a night.

33

ROBESPIERRE: (*Mutters.*) You make me sick.

DANTON: And vice versa, my friend. Nothing – nothing more sickening than an entirely honest man. Not an ounce of understanding for the rest of us – who do you think you are – God? Roast in hell for your arrogance.

ROBESPIERRE is stricken by the truth of this.

DANTON: (*Relenting.*) Anyway, it don't work. Impose virtue by force and your vice will ooze out sideways.

ROBESPIERRE: You doom us all to criminality then?

DANTON: Didn't say that. Must have a system... reward ingenuity, punish the idle.

ROBESPIERRE: Carrot and stick? Conditional love?

DANTON: What's love got to do with it?

ROBESPIERRE gets up, moves carefully to exit.

ROBESPIERRE: This meeting has been a mistake.

DANTON: What's the matter? What's up?

ROBESPIERRE: Nothing. You make me sick. (*He goes.*)

DANTON: Maxime!

DANTON, furious, lurches to his feet, exits.

STANISLAWA: (*Murmurs.*) Danton, furious, exits! 'You make me sick.' That's good. (*She prowls, pokes the fire.*)

A rat-a-tat-tat on the door. STANISLAWA is startled. Another knock. She watches in alarm as the latch is gently lifted. The door opens and ANNA looks in. She is young, well-dressed in a crimson coat with a fur neck piece and a fetching fur hat. She carries a basket. STANISLAWA tries to block the way but ANNA slides past her with a warm smile. Which fades as she takes in the room.

STANISLAWA: What can I do for you?

ANNA: But... (*She looks round, her manners forgotten.*) How do you live? Where do you sleep?

STANISLAWA: Was there something you wanted?

ANNA: I... my husband thought... (*She still looks round compulsively, her head craning this way and that, her eyes wide.*) ... we – dinner. We thought if you would come to dinner. There's no need to walk – my husband has a car now, it's outside... we have a chauffeur! (*Excited, she takes STANISLAWA by the arm and forces her to the door, impelling her outside.*)

(*Outside.*) Do you like the colour? I chose it, we were going to have red but blue is my favourite.

(*As they come in again.*) Do you like the wine upholstery?

STANISLAWA nods abruptly. Silence. The sight of the room again makes ANNA falter. But she braces herself.

ANNA: You can't stay here – you can't!

But STANISLAWA crosses and stands by the door to see her out.

ANNA: Please, won't you come?

She approaches, smiling, and puts a grey-gloved hand on STANISLAWA's arm. STANISLAWA is slightly mesmerised by her warmth, her scent, her clothes.

ANNA: My Father-in-law sent us a brace of pheasant – nothing formal... no need to... (*Again she trails off with a covert glance at STANISLAWA's appearance.*) Please... we know so few people in Gdansk and you were so kind about the dog. Jaroslav's found some books that might interest you. About the French Revolution.

STANISLAWA: Who by? Jaurès? Aulard? Mathiez?... the new Marxist stuff?

ANNA: Oh heaven knows... I'm afraid I don't have time for reading. (*She puts her hand on STANISLAWA's arm again.*) Please. Just a nice warm supper, and we'll drive you back, in the car...

STANISLAWA wavers, mainly because ANNA's smile is genuinely warm and infectious. She nods briefly, removes the sack from her shoulders. ANNA watches, fascinated, smiles encouragingly and turns for a last glance at the room, to take everything in, for her friends.

ANNA: There'll just be my sister-in-law and our colleagues the Krassowskis – and... (*Triumphant.*) ... the Deputy Headmaster and his godson are looking in to listen to our gramophone.

STANISLAWA, aghast, stops in her tracks.

ANNA: No?

STANISLAWA shakes her head briefly.

ANNA: Can't I tempt you? There's a nice warm fire – huge logs, we could bring back some wood in the car –

STANISLAWA: Thank you, no. Good night.

ANNA sulks.

ANNA: My husband said you wouldn't. (*She pouts, having lost her bet.*) Well. Anyway... (*She proffers the basket.*) There's a meat pie and some sausage, and a winter pudding.

STANISLAWA: Thank you, I have provisions.

ANNA stands, embarrassed, holding out the basket.

STANISLAWA: You mustn't keep your car waiting. It'll get cold.

ANNA: Oh, yes! (*She looks outside, puts the basket and the milk on the table hurriedly and goes, with a wave of her gloved hand.*)

STANISLAWA: You've forgotten your groceries!

She lobs the basket out of the door. Energised, she wheels back and walks about muttering, her arms wrapped about her for warmth.

STANISLAWA: Winter pudding!

"Poor thing!... and here am I, a warm, cosy bunny with my man and my little bunnies and my things to define me, all my muffs and ruffles and aren't I the bee's knees, who can take his eyes off me I'm the crystallised violet of Gdansk, perhaps I'll even let him tonight, ooh he's given me a rash, would you like to see my portrait?"

(*She sits, exhausted.*) God murder every coquette in this world, every bourgeois female renegade to decency.

She sits, gazing into the fire. Music. Enter WAITER.

STANISLAWA: (*Dreamily.*) *He* bought me pheasant.

Not the first time. The first time we had lamb. Smoked herring in a sour sauce and then lamb, with spring cabbage. And he didn't like sweet things. (*Enter FATHER.*)

STANISLAWA: Don't you like sweet things?

Her FATHER is sitting at the table. She sits across from him, leans over and inspects his dinner plate.

STANISLAWA: It doesn't look as though you like any of it. Do you mind?

She takes his plate, scrapes his food on to her own and eats, her head down with pleasure. After a few mouthfuls she looks up.

STANISLAWA: First thing I've eaten since I left Aunt Helena's.

(*He regards her through cigar smoke.*) Helena. Mum's sister. (*Her mouth full.*) I've lived with her since I was eleven.

She's lovely. (*Leans across the table confidentially.*) Married to an idiot.

She finishes. The WAITER refills their glasses. STANISLAWA blows out her cheeks, enjoying being full, and warm, and with him. She glances at him covertly, with avid appreciation.

STANISLAWA: Do you remember my Mother?

He looks at her through the smoke, drawing on his cigar.

STANISLAWA: She was a painter.

Name of Pajak. Aniela.

It doesn't matter.

(*She laughs.*) I was afraid you'd be ashamed of me – this is the only dress I've got.

He inspects her appearance, sucks his teeth.

STANISLAWA: What I'd really like is a new hat. Red – offensive!

She sits back and looks around the restaurant, amazed.

STANISLAWA: Sensational. Everybody here looks famous... beautiful... utterly unique!

She empties her glass. He refills it at once and she lifts it high.

STANISLAWA: To Warsaw... the Queen of cities!

He lifts his glass. STANISLAWA licks the wine from her lips, looks around again and then leans towards him.

STANISLAWA: Is my neck as long as my Mother's?

He thinks, lifting his head.

She looks at the other diners.

STANISLAWA: I'd like a choker of rubies, no, fire opals, foiled with silver to make them glow. (*Getting drunk.*) I want to look Mexican, sensational!

He gives her a sneering look.

She jumps, startled, then laughs, delighted as the restaurant band breaks into a noisy Polish dance.

STANISLAWA: Oh!! (*She jumps up.*) I'm going to dance, dance, dance till my ankles crack and my feet fall off then I'll hop, hop, hop on my bones till they're polished ivory stumps and I'll earn my living making holes for fences and buy my own clothes and sail to Madagascar!

She dances to the music. Her FATHER rises and dances, circling her, his arms high. When the music stops he lifts her high in his arms, part of the dance. She laughs, triumphant. But as he lets her down he holds her, close. She releases herself, embarrassed and he falls flat on his back.

STANISLAWA: Papa? Father?

Her FATHER is out cold. She tries to lift him, looks round for assistance.

STANISLAWA: Can you help me?

The WAITER comes forward indolently, cigarette in mouth.

WAITER: He's finished for tonight. Do you want to go through his pockets?

STANISLAWA: You fool, he's my Father. He's just drunk.

WAITER: Not all he is. Watch out.

She glares at him ferociously. The WAITER removes his uniform. It is ST. JUST. He kicks the FATHER.

ST. JUST: (*Mutters.*) Kill Danton – kill Danton. (*Heaves the FATHER offstage.*)

STANISLAWA: What?

STANISLAWA dozes in the armchair.

ANNA, in another elegant ensemble, knocks, sees that STANISLAWA is asleep, slips in circumspectly, and leaves food. She looks round the room, crosses herself and goes, glad to leave such a place.

STANISLAWA notices the food without surprise, forages laconically, and eats the first thing that comes to hand without inspecting it. But eating sets off memories.

STANISLAWA: He gave me carp. And wild boar.

And green lizard shoes with extremely high heels.

She has another forage, takes a drink from the basket. It fortifies her.

STANISLAWA: Mmmm...

Indians drink their own piss. I wonder how that started – 'Ah, lemonade, thanks, I'm feeling thirsty... mmm, yes, smells familiar, can't quite place the taste.'

(*Pacing.*) Maxime... the virtuous man.

Virtue. And is virtue truth – is truth virtue?

(*Turning it over.*) Truth. As reality.

And how is truth... how is reality, pray, related to love? (*She grimaces to heaven.*)

Through mercy? Loving mercy? No, no, no, no, can't – that's the old God... Christ, I know Nothing!.. I don't know Anything. (*She calls heavenwards.*) Some of us don't know very much! We're dense! Help... do something!

Huh.

Demoted.

The scene changes to her FATHER's apartment in Warsaw. She pours schnapps into shot glasses, awaiting her FATHER's return, and turning over ideas for her play on the French Revolution.

STANISLAWA: Robespierre, respecting Danton for his animal courage, his generosity of spirit, his revolutionary achievements... detesting his greed, his smiling, calculating deviousness...

The door bangs and her FATHER is there, a looming, ominous figure in his greatcoat. He throws it off and she takes it before it hits the floor, is ready with his glass of schnapps as he slumps heavily into a chair, drawing on his cigar.

STANISLAWA: Schnapps?

He downs it in one, lifts his hand and she is ready with the next glass.

He belches, ignores her. She stands, watching him hopefully. But her presence is ignored.

STANISLAWA: (*At last.*) Do you... mm... (*He swivels round at her, his gaze cold.*) ... do you love me?

FATHER: (*His face frightening.*) What?

STANISLAWA: No, why should you, there's no reason why you should, we're strangers.

I always knew.

That I was somebody.

Mother was talented, but never to the hilt.

Whenever she got somewhere, she stopped! Put her foot through the canvas and started again.

FATHER: Frightened of her own shit.

STANISLAWA: But not us. We're alike, aren't we? Artists.

41

He seems half-asleep.

STANISLAWA: Everything to the utmost. True Poles. (*Laughs.*) More schnapps?

She pours schnapps.

STANISLAWA: Same at school. (*He looks at her briefly.*) The nuns. (*His eyes flicker with interest at 'nuns'.*) Coming at you with eyes like a furnace – 'God is Love, God is Love!' 'Listen' I said. 'I don't want love – I want justice.' Good communist dogma, that.

She finishes her drink, unaware that he is watching her like a predator. Catching his gaze, she grins.

STANISLAWA: Nuns! (*She prances.*)

FATHER: Turn around, let's have a look at you.

She is pleased at this attention. She turns, smiling. He gazes up at her, unblinking. She is held, then feels suddenly odd. She giggles.

STANISLAWA: I've been trying to read your books – hopeless, I'm useless at the avant-garde, I must have a literal mind.

Unnerved by his gaze, she squats at his feet, like a child.

STANISLAWA: (*Cross-legged, gazing up at him.*) You know what you are.

He prods her with his foot.

STANISLAWA: An explorer!

You don't Map jungles, you create them!... chaotic new worlds! (*Waggles his foot fondly.*) You're so Deep!

He exhales smoke, does not reply.

STANISLAWA: You could give me some help. Say something. (*Clutches his leg, mock-dramatic.*) Speak to me! (*And moves back, facing him, like an obedient pupil.*)

Her FATHER looks at her appraisingly.

FATHER: You're filling out.

She is suddenly furious.

STANISLAWA: You know what you are.

No reply.

STANISLAWA: You're a devil.

He turns, eyes gleaming, almost a smile.

STANISLAWA: You despise everything – you treat everyone, everything with contempt... no, it's not even contempt. Nothing so warm.

Phenomena, that's all we are to you. Objects.

FATHER: (*Gestures to her table.*) Stick to your rubbish.

STANISLAWA: The French Revolution is NOT RUBBISH! It's where we all began – the People!

He gives her a mocking laugh.

STANISLAWA: Oh I don't count you – you're from the carboniferous layer. This play is going to make me famous like you. And rich. So rich I'll be able to buy you new trousers, those are green with piddle stains, people can't take their eyes from your crutch.

He laughs, very loud. Encouraged, she crosses, sits on the arm of his chair and inspects him, peering into his face and examining it minutely.

STANISLAWA: God, map of Waterloo! – where did you get that scar, it's down to the bone... you're all pock marks and purple veins. Keep still. (*She leans over him and squeezes a blackhead on his cheek.*) Hold still, it's huge.

He puts his hand up to the spot, rubbing it. She takes his hand, peruses it.

43

STANISLAWA: Another lab specimen.

She strokes his hand. He watches, then takes her hand and kisses it with mock gallantry.

STANISLAWA: My ugly angel. (*Laughing.*)

He lifts both her hands, kisses the inkstains and then begins to lick them.

STANISLAWA: Don't.

She moves away from him, crosses, sits at her writing table and picks up her pencil. Her FATHER watches her, drink in hand. She looks across at him, ignores him, writes rapidly. He gets up, looms over her shoulder, picks up one of her books, reads, throws it down.

FATHER: (*Sneering.*) Robespierre?

STANISLAWA: A brilliant and virtuous man whose influence is only now beginning to be –

FATHER: (*Leans over, breathing into her face.*) That masochist?

STANISLAWA: The French Revolution was the beginning of –

FATHER: Danton's balls... that's what he needed, your eunuch. You want a revolution, you want a Danton. (*He breathes over her, teetering slightly.*)

STANISLAWA: (*Looks up at him bleakly.*) No you don't.

FATHER: Why not?

STANISLAWA: Because they're the same. Robespierre and Danton. Men. Wanting blood. And then sick of it. Men like to kill. Experience killing. Until they do it. Then it's too late. The damage is done.

FATHER: (*Jeers.*) And women?

STANISLAWA: Women bleed anyway.

FATHER: So not such a hero, your Robespierre?

STANISLAWA: Even more a hero. He saw the truth.

FATHER: Truth? Huh! (*Stabs a finger on her page.*) You want a revolution, you want a man! You know what a man is, don't you?

She rises, to confront him. It looks as though he may strike her, but he turns, knocking her over, swipes up his coat and goes... knocking over a chair.

STANISLAWA: (*Righting the chair, calls after him.*) Pig! You're a pig! I know all about Danton!

She crosses and sits at her table.

(*Writes rapidly, speaking aloud.*) Now it's a stalking match. Paris is anarchy. Factions form by the day. One fact is clear... to the Convention, to the Committees... to Paris itself. Control must be established and established by one man. It must be Robespierre – or Danton.

ROBESPIERRE enters swiftly, followed by ST. JUST.

ST. JUST: Maxime, make up your mind! You must know the danger you're in!

ROBESPIERRE sits, eyes on his papers.

ST. JUST: Face it. We cannot lose France – all our effort, endeavour... because you find a man charming!

ROBESPIERRE: That is cynical. Antoine, I begin to suspect you find no virtue in anyone.

ST. JUST: I must confess there are moments when I doubt the notion of goodwill... sacrifice.

ROBESPIERRE: Rubbish, a Mother will give her life to protect her child.

ST. JUST: Animal instinct.

ROBESPIERRE: You've never known a man die for his friend... his dog... his horse? If there were no feelings beyond the self-concerned, would society have emerged to its present mutual dependence? Man would still forage as predator in the chaos of jungle... or be as extinct as the dinosaur. By asking less, you diminish man to the mean creature you despise. You want me to remove Danton. Whose head will you demand next – mine?

ST. JUST: (*Shocked.*) Maxime!

ROBESPIERRE: (*Milder.*) You must see the dangers within, as well as without.

ST. JUST: (*After a pause.*) It doesn't alter the fact. Danton is a thug. He grows meaner and more dangerous by the day. You believe in human virtue. Do me the courtesy of conceding human vice. You are surrounded by it.

(*He sits, drags his chair close to ROBESPIERRE.*) The Terror has been instituted, not for mere revenge, but for control. Without control we are open to the most savage exploitation. Better the ancien regime than that.

The use of Terror has been sanctioned by the Convention. Have the statesmanship to use it. He will have you if you don't.

Silence.

ROBESPIERRE: I am seeking to preserve, not destroy.

Yes, Danton's a venal man – but he knows it. He respects me. I can't afford the luxury of more heads in the gutter.

ST. JUST rises in fury. He sweeps up his papers and jacket.

ST. JUST: Paris will never forgive you. (*Goes.*)

ROBESPIERRE: (*Calls.*) We need his voice.

ROBESPIERRE exits.

STANISLAWA writes with increasing rapidity for a long moment. Silence, but for the rustle of paper as she covers swift pages. An atmosphere of rapt serenity. A letter drops through the door. She reads it aloud.

STANISLAWA: '... my dear, again no word from you. Even your in-love-with-his-own-importance Uncle looked in the letterbox this morning... probably to see if his elevation to the Nobility had arrived... anyway, dear heart, here's a little money for food and fuel... (*STANISLAWA opens the letter to enjoy the sight of the money... reads on.*) ... Pani Nowicka did a pattern for my dress with the new neckline – what do you think... (*STANISLAWA looks at the sketch, laughs.*) ... will it excite the church choir too much, I don't want to cause seizures. (*STANISLAWA laughs.*)

'How is your dreadful Père – demonic as ever? Keep away, dearest. He is not a good person. I must stop now, I have a sheep's head to pickle – no, FOR your Uncle – the only man in Cracow who thought a lemon had legs and squeezed a canary into his schnapps.'

STANISLAWA: (*Murmurs.*) Ohh... schnapps!

She looks up at the noise of her FATHER's entrance. She rises and backs away as he lurches towards her, drunk and dangerous.

FATHER: Get out.

STANISLAWA: What's the matter?

FATHER: Get out!

Silence. STANISLAWA is shocked.

STANISLAWA: I haven't anywhere to go.

He crosses to the door, re-enters with a WOMAN.

STANISLAWA: Oh. I'm sorry. I –

But she stands, shocked, unable to move. The WOMAN whispers to her FATHER, who begins to grope at her. Ignoring STANISLAWA, they embrace noisily. Then the WOMAN pulls away.

WOMAN: What about the money, where's the money? Bastard!

He cracks her across the face, begins to rip her clothes off. But the WOMAN fights back, clouts him over the head. He reels. The WOMAN sees AUNT HELENA's money, takes it, makes her escape, but he follows her. Sounds of the fight outside the door... screams and shouts... her FATHER's hoarse swearing, then the sounds die away to silence.

STANISLAWA stands. Her FATHER enters. His head is bleeding from a head wound, and the blood is running down his face. STANISLAWA bursts out laughing.

STANISLAWA: Hah... borscht soup!

She throws him a cloth for the blood.

STANISLAWA: Serves you right.

She takes a prudent step back as his head rears up.

STANISLAWA: Oh, you devil... you love it, don't you? (*Cleans his face.*) You're a devil, d'you know that?

And she clasps him to her protectively. He lifts her onto his lap, covers her with tender kisses.

STANISLAWA: (*Laughing.*) No... no! Wrong woman!

But he kisses her on the mouth. She slides down, backs away from him.

STANISLAWA: It's me, Stanislawa... what are you kissing ME for?

He begins to stalk her.

There is a prolonged, silent tussle. Then he traps her. And throws her down, lifting her clothes and forcing her legs open. She makes a last, despairing effort to escape. He puts a hand on her neck, half-throttling her. And then reaches out, taking up an empty wine bottle.

She shrieks, one awful howling shriek.

End of Act One.

ACT TWO

AUNT HELENA has come to help STANISLAWA move in.
STANISLAWA sits, white-faced. STANISLAWA rises, moves.
HELENA observes her shrewdly.

HELENA: (*Observing STANISLAWA alertly.*) Are you on
morphine?

> *STANISLAWA looks across at her with a level stare.*

HELENA: When did you start?

> Never mind. We'll wait until you feel more like yourself.
> (*STANISLAWA shakes her head violently, turns away.*)

> You should have let me go to law. You could at least have
> had justice.

STANISLAWA: Justice? Hardly a luxury available to a
bastard.

HELENA: You will survive. Trust me.

STANISLAWA: No. (*She turns with a sudden, frightening
violence, reaches out as HELENA steps back, lifts a plate high
and drops it. It smashes.*) Finished.

HELENA: (*Picking up the pieces.*) That's not true. Trample a
plant, it springs up again... sun, water, the right soil...
(*As STANISLAWA shakes her head.*) ... ohh, what a Pole
you are! Learn to bend! (*As she delves in her large canvas
bag.*) Where is he, by the way? Your Father.

STANISLAWA: Gone to Posnan.

HELENA: What for?

STANISLAWA: I don't know! To frighten the women and
children I suppose.

She gives STANISLAWA soup from a thermos. STANISLAWA sips.

HELENA: You're as mad as he is.

STANISLAWA: Well, I'm his daughter! (*But the soup makes her feel better.*)

You don't understand.

All my life, until I found him, I was in the wrong place. The wrong planet. I kept waiting – waiting for it all to stop – for my own life... MY life, to begin.

HELENA: Oh my dear.

STANISLAWA: What?

HELENA: Don't you know? I thought you knew.

STANISLAWA: What?

HELENA: All women feel that. In the centre of things, but exiled.

STANISLAWA: (*Looks at HELENA. She sips the hot soup.*) I used to dream about him. My Father. This magical Nordic man, I thought... at least, until one day at school in Paris, we started on the French Revolution.

I couldn't take it in. All these amazing people – a whole country – believing that it was possible to start again, make an entirely new society – (*HELENA smiles.*) think of it – to rule not by power but by decency! (*HELENA listens.*) Oh I know it only lasted a couple of years – that came as a shock –

HELENA: Too fast. Poor husbandry, I call it.

STANISLAWA: Yes, but what they achieved!

HELENA: While they had their heads.

STANISLAWA: New criminal codes, equality before the law, trial by jury! Nepotism abolished, freedom for Protestants and Jews, education out of the hands of the Church... Robespierre even wanted the right to fair employment! I couldn't stop talking, I tried to tell people how phenomenal it all was – of course nobody listened. At school they thought I was cracked and who else was there to tell?

HELENA: Your Mother?

STANISLAWA: When I wasn't hiding the bottles. It didn't matter. None of it mattered. I wasn't alone any more. HE was there.

HELENA: Your hero...

STANISLAWA: Maximilien Robespierre. I couldn't believe it. Everything I thought... his thoughts. I felt... stable.

HELENA unwraps waxed paper, offers STANISLAWA an iced cake. She takes it and bites, murmuring with pleasure. She wipes her mouth, relaxes in the chair, head back.

STANISLAWA: (*Dreamily.*) Sometimes... when we were in the money... my Mother would splash out. Once in Venice new clothes from the skin out – hats, shoes, handbags, we spent a fortune on costumes for Carnival, she was with this Armenian, in tungsten. The Lido, the Opera, gondolas... it was as if we were in a spell.

Only there was this beggar. With no nose. You kept seeing him – Venice is a small place.

Another time, on the Riviera, one of her lovers had built a hotel – all glass and marble, you would have hated it. There was this injured dog, under my window at the back where the garden hadn't been made up. He howled, all the time. Nobody took a blind bit of notice and in the end I couldn't stand it and said couldn't something be

done, so one of the waiters hit him on the head with a
spade. In front of me. And waited for a tip.

HELENA: Oh! Killed it?

STANISLAWA: (*Shakes her head.*) It crawled off into the
pines. I could hear the noises for two days but
I couldn't find him. Then they stopped.

How can you enjoy yourself?

*ST. JUST enters with ROBESPIERRE, is alarmed at the
sight of him.*

ST. JUST: Please – you must rest.

ROBESPIERRE: (*Mutters.*) How can I stop when so much
is unbearable?

ST. JUST: At least you'll be safe now.

ROBESPIERRE: Safe?

ST. JUST: Danton will be where he belongs, where all
animals belong – in a cage. Your signature please.
There. (*Points.*)

*There is a long pause. It looks as if ROBESPIERRE will
not sign. But eventually he picks up a pen and scratches the
parchment. ST. JUST grasps the paper swiftly.
ROBESPIERRE finds it hard not to collapse. He supports
himself on his hand as ST. JUST goes, smiling in triumph.
ROBESPIERRE exits.*

*STANISLAWA is suddenly overcome with laughter. She
cannot stop, stuffs her skirt into her mouth. HELENA
watches, not knowing whether to smile or be alarmed at this
outburst.*

STANISLAWA: You know... (*Laughter.*) ... in my mind...
this... Hero!

(*Peals with laughter.*) Those books!

HELENA: You read them?

STANISLAWA: Dreadful! So bad... Lies, all of them!

HELENA: You must forget him, my dear. Put him out of your mind.

STANISLAWA: At least he's not boring.

HELENA: He did his best to murder you.

STANISLAWA: (*Suddenly vicious.*) Leave my Father alone!

HELENA: He's a monster!

STANISLAWA: The rules are different for him. You don't understand.

HELENA: Understand what? Mystical rubbish about being an artist? Normal rules please ignore? He's flawed! A monster! He thinks there's no God, that he's on his own, that he can do as he likes, and survive. All right. He is your Father. You found him. Now let go. We have to survive our parents.

STANISLAWA rises, stands before HELENA.

STANISLAWA: You have such a clear mind.

HELENA: Survive. For me.

STANISLAWA: For the work. Work, work, work, work, work. To the utmost.

She gets out the morphine.

HELENA: My dear, do you need that?

STANISLAWA: Oh yes. It releases the mind wonderfully.

HELENA watches STANISLAWA take the morphine, sighs, puts on her hat and coat, kisses STANISLAWA tenderly, and goes.

STANISLAWA sits in a dream.

STANISLAWA: (*Murmurs.*) There must be SOME excitement...

DANTON enters, vigorous and alive in a greatcoat. He dashes the rain from his hat, takes off his coat, throws it down.

DANTON: My God... (*He laughs, excited, looks out of the window, breathes deeply.*) ... the air! Ohh! The first night of spring... I could pleasure the world!

He strides back and forth, unable to keep still, smirks briefly at STANISLAWA, then returns to the window, surveying the scene below him.

DANTON: (*Softly.*) Well, Paris... are you mine?

STANISLAWA indicates that LOUISE has appeared.

DANTON: Louise! Beloved! There you are...

But LOUISE crosses below him, candelabrum held high.

DANTON: Where are you going?

LOUISE: To the chapel. To pray.

Leaps down to her.

DANTON: Pray? – for Georges Danton? (*Laughing.*) He's not finished yet! (*She moves away.*) Come here, let me look at you. (*He takes the candelabrum from her.*) Ohhh... (*He touches her; she resists.*)

LOUISE: Don't! I don't want to...

DANTON: What's the matter, don't you want me... doesn't she want her husband?

LOUISE: (*Breaks away.*) No...

DANTON: (*Sinks to his knees.*) Please...

LOUISE: I'm pregnant!

How can I carry a child? I'm not ready yet!

He buries his head in her stomach, looks up and smiles at her, full of lust.

DANTON: I'll be very gentle... I'll hardly go inside.

(*Tougher.*) What's the matter, you'll enjoy it.

She spits in his face, looks at him with loathing, from a safe distance.

LOUISE: You really think a woman goes with an old man for pleasure!?

DANTON: I've been very patient with...

LOUISE: You bought me! Like a dog on a string! When was I asked? Who consulted me? I can wait...

DANTON: What for?

LOUISE: Every time you slander Robespierre, and sneer, and ridicule him, – I know he's won! – taken one more day away from you. And I thank God for it!

DANTON: You should have kept your mouth shut. (*He laughs suddenly.*) A Robespierre? Demolish a Danton!

What do you know of the world! You think I can't turn Paris in a night! I'll make you a present. Crush the little reptile, and give you his bones for an eggtimer.

The sound of marching feet and a knock at the door. They freeze. ST. JUST enters. They freeze in shock, then ST. JUST, tense, bows, proffers a paper.

DANTON: (*Dismissive.*) Not now, boy.

DANTON turns away, snubbing him, so LOUISE takes the document.

LOUISE: What is it?

DANTON: (*Mutters.*) Leave it, it's nothing!

ST. JUST: (*Wiretight.*) I have the honour to present, Citizen Danton, the warrant for your arrest.

LOUISE: (*She gasps, then whispers.*) Yes!!

STANISLAWA: (*Echoes at the same time.*) YES!!

ST. JUST: On behalf of the Committee of Security and the Convention of the Revolution. My compliments.

DANTON: They – don't – dare!

ST. JUST inclines his head. LOUISE sweeps up DANTON's coat and thrusts it at him. DANTON grabs LOUISE and embraces her roughly. She holds out the coat again. DANTON turns his back on her and goes to the door, and turns to her...

DANTON: Expect me back within the hour!

They both look at him. DANTON smiles gaily. She thrusts his coat towards him. He will not take it. ST. JUST takes the coat brusquely, indicates for DANTON to leave. It looks as though DANTON will strike him, but then he smiles again, a wide, sickening smile, and sweeps out. ST. JUST looks keenly at LOUISE, who stands like a statue, then moves to the window, to see them leave below. She goes out with the candelabrum held high.

STANISLAWA, from her table, observes ST. JUST and ROBESPIERRE.

ROBESPIERRE: (*To ST. JUST.*) You've been down to the Convention?

ST. JUST: I've just come from the floor.

ROBESPIERRE: And?

ST. JUST: Hostility and confusion. But once the air is cleared, oh!... everything possible!

STANISLAWA smiles at him disbelievingly. He jumps onto the table.

ST. JUST: Maxime! Can't you smell it... the new century, so close! Think of it – a new age. An age of science... reason. Imperialism as dead as Attila the Hun.

STANISLAWA: That easily?

ST. JUST: By the stroke of the pen. Aristocracy, privilege of random birth, all removed – by edict.

STANISLAWA: You believe it, that the lawyers will rule the world?

ST. JUST: Justice –

STANISLAWA: Ah, well, justice. And who will enforce your justice? The warriors whose tents you've burned? Whose honour you deride?

ST. JUST: Honour? Medieval superstition. The impulse to suicide. There must be force... yes... to protect us... a properly organised body of men devoted to just aims and –

STANISLAWA: They'll be needed. (*She sits, as if defeated.*)

ST. JUST: Maxime! (*Softly.*) Courage! (*To ROBESPIERRE, fierce.*) You cannot turn back now.

ROBESPIERRE: (*Looks up at him.*) Oh I don't intend to.

ST. JUST: He must be eliminated.

ROBESPIERRE: I agree.

ST. JUST: I'm glad to hear it. Every stone in the path of –

ROBESPIERRE: (*Waves a hand.*) Please. I shall kill Danton because if I do not, he will kill me.

ST. JUST: Thank God. His ambition –

ROBESPIERRE: Not even ambition. He truly believes himself to be the better choice.

ST. JUST: Hah! The degree of self-delusion alone denotes a lesser –

ROBESPIERRE: Antoine!... how can Georges Danton... lover of women... allow himself to be dominated by a man with a smaller member than himself?

ST. JUST: Primitive!

STANISLAWA: He would say human.

ST. JUST: At all events, behind bars.

ROBESPIERRE: If we can keep him there. (*Laughs quietly, ST. JUST frowns in enquiry.*) 'You have one bad card Georges.' (*ST. JUST shakes his head, puzzled.*)

Searches his papers.

ROBESPIERRE: From his diary. Discovered in the search of his rooms. (*Reads aloud.*) 'In the glorious spring of '94, Danton's heart, because Danton was a man, turned, despite affairs of state, to thoughts of love – to lovers, touching, speaking the soft, tender filth between a man and a woman...'

ST. JUST: A romantic. Splendid. He can die for love, we'll make him martyr of the revolution.

STANISLAWA: He won't see that as his role.

ST. JUST: Because he thinks he's going to win?

ROBESPIERRE: Are we so sure that he won't? (*Goes to the door. Sounds of pandemonium.*)

STANISLAWA: (*As LEGENDRE.*) Friends... members of the Convention! Permission to speak... permission to speak!

Citizen Legendre demands the floor.

We have just been shocked and outraged to learn that members of this government have, this night, been arrested...

STANISLAWA writes swiftly.

STANISLAWA: (*As LEGENDRE.*) ... we hear that one of the accused is Citizen Danton! (*Reaction.*) Comrades... brothers... I move that those who have been arrested are permitted to answer charges against them on the floor of this Chamber. They deserve, they have earned... the right of reply. (*Reaction.*)

ROBESPIERRE and ST. JUST look at each other.

ROBESPIERRE: (*Addressing the audience – shrill, against the noise.*) I request the right to speak... I request the right to speak! (*He stands, immobile, waits a long time for the noise on the P/A to die down.*)

(*Mildly.*) It's a long time, gentlemen, since we began our sitting with such a display of temper. (*He pauses, looks around.*) Today... today we shall see what we value more – the Republic – or the individual.

STANISLAWA: We'll see if you deserve to rule, tyrant!

ROBESPIERRE: (*Looks across at her coolly.*) I will raise that point too. (*He waits for silence on the P/A.*)

Citizen Legendre demands that the accused be allowed to answer charges from this floor. (*Shouts of agreement. He raises his voice.*) Are you saying – are you saying that you wish to accord to those now under arrest privileges that have been denied those preceding them? If Citizen Legendre believes in special consideration then that is a mistake which we must correct in him. It is not the function of a revolutionary Convention to grant privilege. That is what we are here to abolish. (*Silence.*)

STANISLAWA: (*As LEGENDRE.*) To hear the accused from this floor is not privilege, it's simple justice!

And you watch out – the fall of Danton will crush you to pieces! (*Noise.*)

STANISLAWA: Citizen Robespierre?

He nods at her briefly, again waits for silence.

ROBESPIERRE: If... if by some mystic law the destruction of criminality should bring about my ruin, well... what of it?

What is so devastating about that?

Are we... are we to allow private danger to inhibit public decision?

Of course not.

He pauses, and looks about him keenly, as if to note every man present.

ROBESPIERRE: Gentlemen – what are we here for? We are here to create a new society. A society based on the notion of democracy. On the notion of personal freedom – (*A sudden scream.*) No man is born a slave! Another man makes him so! (*Some cheering. He recovers his coolness.*) We mean to build a state without hierarchy, where notions of comfort, dignity and personal happiness are not confined to the few at the expense of the many. You think that impossible? With so much energy locked in want and despair? Wasted in human beings deprived of the means of survival, let alone education, civilisation! I tell you, we have the means to unlock that energy. Here, for the first time in the history of the world, we have a chance to save the world, for the world... for the people of the world... ALL people... everywhere! Must that great work be put at risk? For personal greed? For criminality? I, Maximilien Robespiere – Citizen – say NO!!! (*Cheers.*)

I move that the order for the arrest of the prisoner Danton and his confederates be confirmed.

A roar of agreement. He waits for silence.

ROBESPIERRE: (*Briefly.*) And that the accused be brought to the floor of this house for questioning.

Loud cheering. He allows himself a small smile towards STANISLAWA, picks up his papers and goes.

STANISLAWA collapses on her seat, frozen and exhausted. She tries to rise, half-crawls to the fire, tries to wrench the stretcher off a battered picture for firewood but is too weak. It looks as though she will break down but there are sounds, and two letters are dropped through the door. She lurches to her feet and falls on them, ripping them open and searching, tearing the envelopes apart.

STANISLAWA: No – money!

She screws up the letters violently, throws them down unread. She sits, totally exhausted.

STANISLAWA: (*Recalling letters received.*) ... I'm sorry, my dear, but all my jewellery is gone, I've tried everything... I hope you used the zloties from my little table to buy a warm coat... WHY can't I come and see you... you say you're well but... still nothing from you... what do you mean, how can you ask me not to write, I'm your Aunt!... my dear, if that is what you wish... there was no need for you to... My dear Stanislawa, I am in receipt of your brief note and regret to tell you that the University of Warsaw will not renew your grant. I beg you to attend a sanatorium for the withdrawal of drugs. Sincerely, Your Aunt Helena.

(*Rises, knocking over the chair in fury.*) What is the matter with them!... do they think I'm mad!! It is my right to have the money, I have a right to it, I am an artist, that is what the money is for, do they want proof, what proof do they want? I Work! Till four in the morning!

Is it because I see no-one? What do they want me to do, lead the literary life, inhabit the anal orifices of publishers, literary hostesses?

No, I am not depressed! Nor am I lonely. I am alone in order to work and I cope with loneliness by working. If you inhabited the world that I inhabit, a world of the most potent, the most thrilling thought, then you would not be in the least concerned for my welfare.

I am in a fever, yes. But of excitement, for the work! There is not a character whose nerves are not stretched into red hot wires across chasms of fright – I can hardly stop them disintegrating! (*Slight fade on voice.*)

DANTON enters, throws himself down in a chair, legs out. He is energized. Begins to think out his address to his fellow prisoners/colleagues.

DANTON: Friends...

(*Rises, walks.*) Comrades... I... I, Danton, I alone can save you. So, if you don't want to end up as dog's meat... (*Laughs, but decides on a more sober tack.*)

My friends... a political trial is not a trial. It is a duel. The Government accuses us? Then we accuse the Government... Believe me, comrades, the game's not over yet!

He turns, with a jerk, as he sees STANISLAWA. Recovers at once, gives her a warm and confident smile.

STANISLAWA: Robespierre came to see Desmoulins this morning. (*DANTON shrugs.*) You persuaded Desmoulins not to see him. By that you have sent your friend to his death.

DANTON: What do any of them matter? You think their lives worth one hour of Danton's existence?

STANISLAWA, repelled, draws back but he does not notice.

STANISLAWA: (*Quietly.*) My God.

DANTON: Cut me down like a common conscript? I'll see him choke on his own vomit first.

STANISLAWA: (*Murmurs.*) No.

DANTON: (*To STANISLAWA.*) Watch me face the Tribunal... (*Laughs.*) ... once I let out the roar, bathe them in my loving eyes... carried by acclamation! As I sweep past in triumph shoulder high he'll be stumbling down the steps to perdition – ohh, we'll see his little toes twitch!

STANISLAWA: And then?

DANTON: And then... ohh... and then...

(*He laughs in ecstasy.*) And then...!

Why, Life! Pleasure!

Pourquoi pas?

Why not splendour... processions, music... fine food, fine houses in the most beautiful country in the world, ohh, La Belle France! – I could eat you, every morsel, from the Manche to the Mare Nostrum – oh, my beloved country! And to think I believed myself finished with it all!

(*He turns to her, his eyes shining.*) Danton, finished – with Living?

I want it – now! My Life! All of it, stretching ahead of me till I'm old and tired and quiet... till I'm ready, made my peace, paid my dues, kissed my grandchildren farewell... I Must Have my Life! Christ, I can't wait to get my boots on... I can't wait for the light!

He wraps himself in his cloak and lies down.

STANISLAWA: (*Stands over him.*) You had our trust. We adored you. (*Walks away.*)

A tap at the door.

STANISLAWA: (*Abrupt.*) What?

ANNA sticks a head round the door. She has a basket of food. STANISLAWA looks at her, then at the basket.

STANISLAWA: Put it on the table.

ANNA does so, waits.

STANISLAWA: That's all. You can go.

ANNA gapes, and then smiles, as at a lunatic and goes, clipping the door sharply. This rings round STANISLAWA's head, making her wince.

ROBESPIERRE enters, is helped into a chair by ST. JUST. ST. JUST puts drops from a phial into a glass, gives the medicine to ROBESPIERRE who drinks it, wincing at the taste. He sets the glass down shakily. A knock at the door. ST. JUST goes out, we hear him talking urgently. He re-enters.

ST. JUST: They're waiting for you.

At once ROBESPIERRE is on his feet, smiling and in apparent good health. He sweeps out followed by ST. JUST.

STANISLAWA gasps, trying to pull herself together for work... But her head goes back on the chair.

STANISLAWA: Either you can get me money, get my manuscript typed... or you're of no use to me!!

You're not my Mother! What do you want – gratitude?

You can see how grateful I am! – I'm Working!!

I'm doing what I'm For!

All I want is money for drugs, and a little food.

Don't keep sending letters!

She picks up her pen, writes a letter to her Aunt.

STANISLAWA: (*Live, writing.*) Helena – I don't want to call you Aunt any more, it's too cloying... please know that

I reserve the ownership of my life exclusively for myself. At the cost of comfort, companionship and dignity.

None of it is important.

She stops writing.

STANISLAWA: It's amazing what you can do without. Were you aware that one can live indefinitely on snow? (*She looks around.*)

If you could see the frosting on the windows! I'm surrounded by jewels! My breath on the air keeps me company, the icicles on the window are my guardians. This is all there is. This and Work.

If you have no money to send, forget me. If necessary I shall beg on the streets.

So please... no more interruption. I have Danton's trial to deal with.

ROBESPIERRE enters quickly, throws himself down at the table as the sound, from several separate sources, rises on the P/A.

STANISLAWA crosses to him urgently and speaks, out of breath, her voice raised against the hubbub on the P/A.

STANISLAWA: Danton's star... is rising by the minute... keep away from the Tribunal, the galleries have gone mad, they're screaming for your blood... you... (*Gasping for breath.*) ... all the Committee, they want to guillotine the lot of us! (*She exits. Noise on the P/A.*)

Silence. ROBESPIERRE plays with a knife on the table.

ROBESPIERRE: (*Looks up.*) I don't know. For the moment I cannot see a way out.

STANISLAWA: (*Reading from letters and urgent notes.*) But our lives are threatened!

We could be dead tomorrow!

We shall have to give in.

We must release Danton at once!

Sign the order now!

You said yourself, what is humiliation where the good of the State is concerned –

ROBESPIERRE: (*To STANISLAWA.*) (*Rises, jams the knife into the table.*) No!!!

(*Silence.*)

That's enough. (*He pauses, then continues in a trembling voice.*)

You think this country can be governed by cringing weakness?

Enter ST. JUST. He fixes ROBESPIERRE with a compelling stare.

ST. JUST: (*To ROBESPIERRE.*) The Tribunal's completely surrounded. Counter-revolutionaries in all the galleries... they've smuggled arms into the building... (*Gasps for breath.*) they're ready to slaughter every deputy in the Chamber...

What are we going to do?

STANISLAWA: Robespierre?

ROBESPIERRE: (*Looks up in cold fury.*) Very well. Your miserable and unimportant lives have been saved for you. (*Raises voice, calls.*) Saint-Just! Take an armed force and surround the building! All citizens found to be carrying arms to be arrested on the spot!

ST. JUST: Thank God. (*He goes swiftly.*)

STANISLAWA: It's all right then?

ROBESPIERRE: No, it is not all right. Now we rule by Terror and Terror alone. (*Groans loudly.*) God knows I never foresaw this.

STANISLAWA: But are we safe?

ROBESPIERRE: (*Looks up, tired.*) For the moment.

ROBESPIERRE rises, then falls back onto his chair.

ROBESPIERRE: I'm sorry. I'm deadly tired. My voice is going. Go down to the floor for me. Tell them – let Danton talk for as long as he wants. But arrest his defence witnesses. Let's see what he is on his own.

STANISLAWA waits restlessly by the window.

DANTON: (*Murmurs.*) Come on... come on...

A sound of steps. A knock. She jumps and ducks under the window. A letter is pushed under the door. She rips it open, looks for money. There is none.

STANISLAWA: Nothing.

Nothing.

Nothing.

Nothing.

Nothing.

(*A pause.*) I must keep the margins straight.

She looks at the pencil stubs on her table.

STANISLAWA: Three left.

I could ask.

I could go to the school.

Go out.

Am I dissolving?

If no-one sees me, do I exist?

Perhaps I am just beginning.

I must...

Dear –

She sits, half-collapses onto the chair with difficulty. All her movements are stiff, slow, erratic, strange.

STANISLAWA: (*Voice-over.*) ... 20, Frimaire... (*Crosses it out.*) – which is the tenth of December, 1928.

Ten below. I can no longer afford a fire.

Odd reactions of the body to cold.

The atmosphere penetrates. All the tissues contract.

Everything grows stiff, like hardening wax.

You can't eat – breaks the teeth. Your tongue, your throat, your palate... You can't swallow. If you do, your stomach won't have it.

You can't think.

But she starts to write. Her chair is at an angle to the table and she cannot straighten it. It takes her a long time even to pick up her pen. But, slowly, she begins to write.

DANTON appears, goes to the dock. His face is savage, his eyes wild. He looks about him, and his look is fearsome.

DANTON: (*To audience.*) You vile, stinking rubbish. You mindless weak-willed ordure... what are you, you braying flock of offal? Oh you'll roar, when some whimpering wretch is being crushed underfoot, that gets your blood going – but Loyalty?!

I know you, you rabble. (*Sounds of laughter.*)

Laugh, would you? When you should be pissing your own blood away for shame? You're spit in the wind... anybody's.

And for what? You? The people? Take over the world? Allow me to make room for you. Félicitations, brothers. You'll be in blood up to your eyeballs.

It's waiting for you – the cart. Can't you hear its wheels creaking – it's waiting for you – yes – you – and you – and you –

And Him!

He'll rot! Smell him – that's him... Maximilien Robespierre... rotting... dissolving... beside the bones of Georges Danton!!!!!!!!

He stumbles out noisily. ROBESPIERRE moves out of the shadows, watches discreetly from the window.

The sound of a crowd approaching. The sound of the wheels of the tumbril on cobblestones. ROBESPIERRE watches, immobile. DANTON can be heard, bellowing.

DANTON: (*As the tumbril passes the window.*) I bequeath you my balls, Robespierre. You'll need them!

The sounds die away slowly. ROBESPIERRE stays by the window.

ROBESPIERRE: (*Murmurs.*) Requiescat in pace.

He staggers as he moves away from the support of the wall by the window.

ROBESPIERRE: (*Murmurs.*) Danton...

With an enormous effort of will he crosses, sits in STANISLAWA's chair and begins to deal with state papers. He works for a prolonged moment, his movements rigid, orderly and precise. She sits at his side, writing.

At last the pile of papers is finished. He puts them in neat files and into folders, ties the folders, straightens his pens, the things on the table, sits up for a still moment, breathes deeply.

ROBESPIERRE: Finished.

STANISLAWA is rigid in her chair, an arm half-raised, still holding a pencil.

He rises, tucks the folders under one arm, removes the pencil from her, puts it on the table, and walks out with a rigid gait.

Silence.

The door is open and there is snow in the room. Snow is banked against the window, covering the panes entirely.

STANISLAWA sits. She is frozen to her chair, her arm frozen in the act of writing, seemingly turned towards ROBESPIERRE's chair in a permanent gaze.

Whiteout.

End of Play.